IMAGES
of America

AROUND THREE MILE BAY

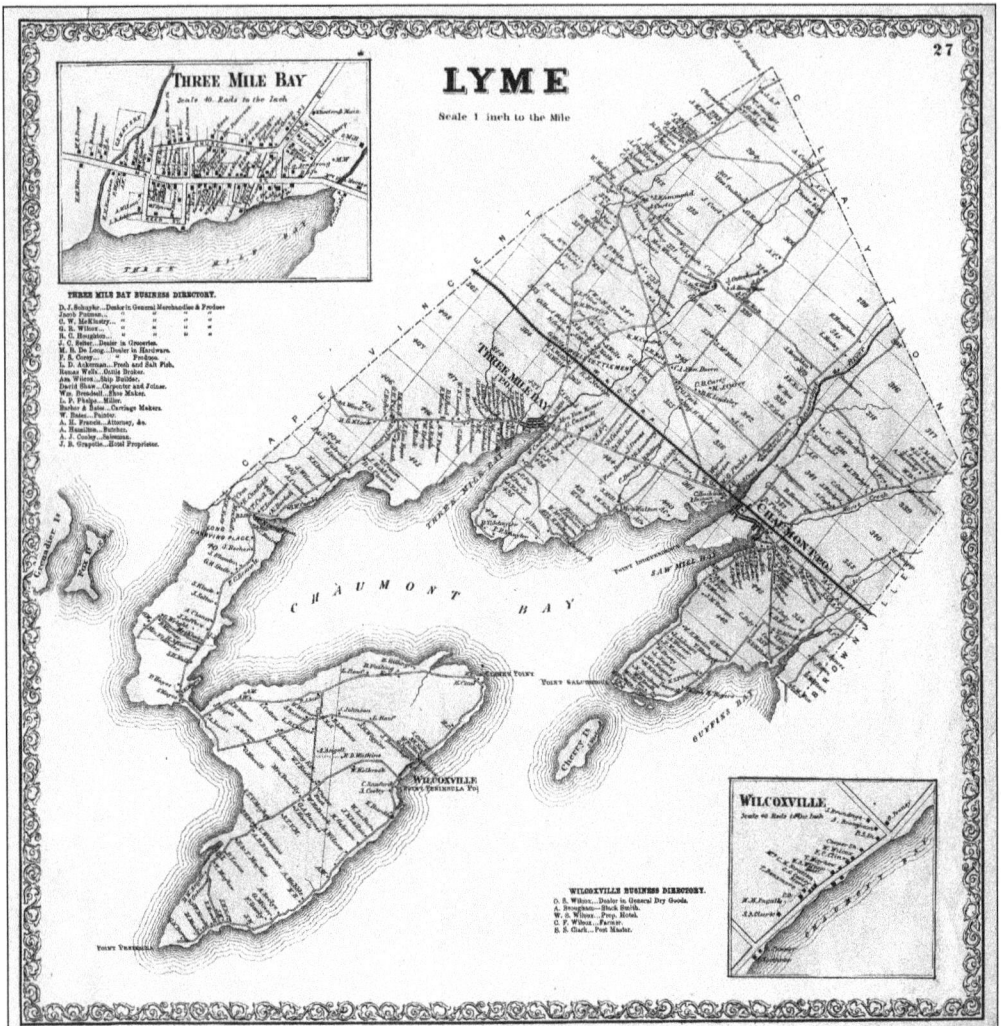

This 1864 map shows the location of the hamlet of Three Mile Bay, the town of Lyme, and the bays. The map is from page 27 of the topographical atlas of Jefferson County created from actual surveys by S. N. and D. G. Beers and Assistants, C. K. Stone Publisher, Philadelphia.

On the cover: Taking a moment to relax while a beautiful view of Three Mile Bay can be seen in the background is Asher Corse, cheese maker at the Three Mile Bay Cheese Factory. (Courtesy of Sharon Clark.)

IMAGES
of America

AROUND THREE MILE BAY

Elaine T. Bock

ARCADIA
PUBLISHING

Published by Arcadia Publishing
Charleston SC, Chicago IL, Portsmouth NH, San Francisco CA

Library of Congress Catalog Card Number: 2008925855

For all general information contact Arcadia Publishing at:
Telephone 843-853-2070
Fax 843-853-0044
E-mail sales@arcadiapublishing.com
For customer service and orders:
Toll-Free 1-888-313-2665

Visit us on the Internet at www.arcadiapublishing.com

CONTENTS

ACKNOWLEDGMENTS

Many people have played a role in the completion of *Around Three Mile Bay*. I appreciate and thank each individually. I hope that everyone will read with pride the completed project. Thank you to my husband, Adam; sons Paul, Richard, and Shawn Norton and daughter-in-law Jessica Norton; Karen Cuppernell; Eileen Bleibtrey; Ann West; Chuck and Polly Yott; Paul and Marilyn Bourcy; Don Lance; John Ahlheim; Marvin and Ann Bourcy; Jeffrey Grant; Sharon Clark; Jack Phillips; Cindy Schreiber; Jeannine Narrigan; Judy Paro; George Cataldo; Lisa Porter at the *Watertown Daily Times*; Betsy and Ed Herrick; Jim Klock; Ted and Sigrid Utess; Lyle and Nancy Weaver; Emelie and Bill Cuppernell; Kent and Mavis Wiley; Rene Gravelle; Mary Lou Garnsey; Don and Betty Reed; Jean and Dick Wiseman; Krista Yott; Eugene Klock; Elsie Lanning; Eleanor VanNess; Jim Kennard; Dan Scoville; the Flower Memorial Library Genealogical Room; the Lyme Central School; and the Jefferson County Historical Society for information, photographs, and support.

INTRODUCTION

Fish and limestone best describe the early years of Three Mile Bay. The hamlet located in Jefferson County got a late start compared to the settlement of Point Peninsula, around 1808; Chaumont, 1801; Three Mile Point, 1816; and other locations in the township of Lyme. The bay, tucked in a small concave valley, is linked to Lake Ontario, which flows into Chaumont Bay, Three Mile Bay, and then branches off into small flowing creeks. Early photographs show the levels of surrounding bodies of water, especially Three Mile Creek, as being extremely higher than those of today.

The waters served the business needs of the community and of master shipbuilder Asa Wilcox, who chose a location for his shipyard that had water depth and the shelter needed for shipbuilding on the water's edge on the south side of the hamlet of Three Mile Bay. Wilcox was considered an excellent craftsman, yet that did not make up for the fact that seafaring vessels under certain circumstances do sink. A recent 2005 discovery beneath Lake Ontario at Oak Orchard/Point Breeze was the wreck of the schooner *Milan*, built by Wilcox at Three Mile Bay in 1845.

Commercial fishing was prominent and at its peak in the late 1880s and continued on into the 1920s, but on a smaller scale. John Lance worked a farm in Three Mile Bay and did commercial fishing as well as making a great number of his own nets. Perl Vosler and Clarence Cheal fished and netted. Throughout the fishing season trout, eels, black bass, and yellow perch were caught in numbers, and at times there would be a lake sturgeon caught in one of the fish nets. Sturgeons weighed in at over 100 pounds and were a worthy catch dollar wise. By 1818, fishing regulations began to be put into effect. The numbers of certain species of fish began to decline. These factors and other added regulations greatly hampered the fishing industry. "Everyone fished" is a quote by Kent Wiley regarding the early years of fishing.

William Dewey was a civil engineer who played an important role in the coming of the railroad. He surveyed and made an estimate in 1838 for the cost associated with extending the route from Watertown to Cape Vincent. When planning for the expansion, the production of northern butter, cheese, woolen products, and flour were added to the equation, making the plan more favorable and feasible. Businesspeople of the region recognized the need for new markets. There were products aplenty to be sold. Smith Barlett, Jerre Carrier, Z. Converse, S. Forsyth, J. DuVillard, T. Peugnet, H. Crevolin, J. T. Ainsworth, F. A. Folger, J. Fellows, D. J. Schuyler, William Carlisle, Isaac Wells, Solon Massey, and Frederick Coffeen formed the committee from Lyme that worked with the Resolutions Committee in the promotion of the rail. The year 1852 saw the first train to travel the tracks past the depot at Three Mile Bay.

Many other residents have played important roles in the development of the area. John B. Taylor, son of John L. Taylor, harness and carriage maker of Three Mile Bay, was responsible for electrical power being brought to the area. The first but not last of his many business ventures was the purchase of the Watertown Gas Company in 1904. He then proceeded to purchase mills and transform them into hydroelectric plants. Ball's Dam on Oswegatchie River was a purchase that resulted in the building of a transmission line to the faltering mills in the village of Edwards. He had the lines extended in 1915 to Edwards and then beyond to Evans Mills, the Thousand Islands, Dexter, Chaumont, Three Mile Bay, Depauville, Clayton, and Alexandria Bay. As each line was extended, Taylor's business absorbed each electric entity along the route: the Electric Company of Chaumont, Cape Vincent Municipal Plant, and those of the Thousand Islands Electric Light Company Clayton, and the electric section of the St. Lawrence Electric Railroad and Land Company of Alexandria Bay.

John J. Barron was an early resident who bought and set up his business in what became known as the Barron Block. He served in many capacities while running a monument business and quarry whose limestone became known as "the best in the state," from this location. John B. Taylor was one of several who noted the quality of the Barron stone and approached Barron with a request to supply it for the upcoming construction of buildings in Watertown and other areas of the country. Stone was used to build the Paddock Arcade, the Watertown National Bank, the Mohican Building, and the House of the Good Samaritan in Watertown, and in the Three Mile Bay area stone was used for bridges, foundations, and buildings as well.

Native limestone has been used in many ways as a construction material. Solid stone slabs have been found covering and lining rock crevice graves of Native Americans who once traveled this northern region. Native American burials such as these were found on Point Peninsula in 1921 by John B. Nichols. Through the years the residents have plowed, dug, and discovered articles that have made their way to the surface at locations on Point Peninsula and other areas in the township of Lyme. There has always been a disagreement about whom these Native Americans really were.

Early settlers came to the area looking for land that had not been settled; they found Three Mile Bay. The accessibility to waterways for travel and food were already available and plentiful. They set up their church and school and began the process of building a community. The hamlet of Three Mile Bay got a late start but prospered.

One

COMMUNITY

This 1950s aerial view shows the hamlet. The bay on the right shows the water vessels that belong to area residents and others that have been launched from Bachy's Marine. The District No. 5 union school appears in the upper left corner of the photograph. When this photograph was taken, the school was still operational. Shown also are the Town Tavern Hotel, the first fire hall, and the Southwell home, lower right. The once bustling hamlet now is a tranquil community. (Courtesy of Jeffrey Grant.)

Young women relax and enjoy the warmth of the afternoon. The house, center, was originally a barn that was brought to its present location from Three Mile Point around 1800. The house on the right was built originally as a summer cottage constructed from old boxes brought from New York Air Brake in Watertown. Houses during this time period were often surrounded by picket fences.

An early constructed native limestone bridge made it possible for the young lady with her fashionable dress and hat to complete the journey over Three Mile Creek. The barn of the Fox farm can be seen in the distance. Barns and farmhouses were a common sight from the 1820s, and John Ross, who was the son of William and Clarissa Whiting Ross, was an expert iron- and woodworker and worked on projects such as this.

The blacksmith shop of Charles Dick opened in the 1890s. Charles helped to meet the needs of the shipping industry and the residents of the community. He was the son of blacksmith Hugh Dick and Johanna Dick. Charles and his wife, Ida P. Maine Dick, left Three Mile Bay in 1908. Charles took the position of superintendent, and Ida became the matron of the old Jefferson County Children's Home located on the corner of Franklin Street and Keyes Avenue in Watertown.

Ken and Edna Bourcy operated the Sunoco gas station until 1986. In 1951, Ken became supervisor of 110 adult and student volunteers that made up the ground observer post for the town of Lyme. This number of aircraft spotters was the largest of any township in Jefferson County. Jack Phillips constructed the building for the observers, which was then moved to the Three Mile Point Main Street location. By 1957, improved radar warning systems made it possible for the air force to relieve observers of their civil defense duties.

In the early 1800s, roads were dirt, not paved. Houses were built along the traffic path. Several past occupants of this street were Claude Mount, Fred Hamilton, Mabel and Claude Herrick, John Ross, and Viola Fish.

The Taylor boathouse was built in 1905 after John B. Taylor had moved the family home from Main Street to the shore of Three Mile Bay. Each owner remodeled the boathouse to suit their own particular taste.

In the 1950s, George Sager took over the Atlantic gas station that had been built on the site of the old mill, a landmark of Three Mile Bay. Claude and Blanche Rickett opened a Shell gas station and restaurant across the street in the limestone building that had housed the Hugh Dick blacksmith shop.

Leon D. Selter ran a farm repair and woodworking shop in 1919. He lived with his wife, Georgia Lott Selter, on the Lott family homestead in Three Mile Point built by Peter Lott in 1838. The long red building stood for many years after the shop was closed.

Mae Mount and her sister Clara housed their skiff in the boathouse on the shoreline of Three Mile Bay. Skiffs and rowboats were a popular form of recreational water transportation during the 1940s. Boating was very popular. Note the circus, bait, and Coke signs, signs of the time period.

The Township Telephone Company in Chaumont was organized in 1907. The Three Mile Bay office was manned by local residents Thelma Ross and Charlotte Nichols. Wesley A. Daniels Jr. was president of the company when modernization shut the office down. The building was razed in 1986, and the property remains vacant. This photograph is of the building just before it was razed.

A stove and tin shop operated on Main Street. J. P. Knowlton, George Rickett, and Page and Company were several stores that fulfilled the tin, stove, and hardware needs of the growing hamlet of Three Mile Bay.

Located on the left side of Main Street, these buildings housed makers of carriages and wagons. The Barber brothers (Mark and William), B. F. Lucas, and C. Simmons were a few that supplied a means of transportation for residents of the area.

This 1800s photograph was taken at the union school in Three Mile Bay. Celebrations with large numbers of people were a common event. This group is not identified.

The Barron Block located on the corner of Main and Depot Streets was built in 1840 for the Day, Cline, and Wilcox Store. The store was operating under the name of Wheeler and Hayes when John J. Barron purchased the building from the Hayes estate to store and sell his marble and granite monuments from.

John J. and Mary Barber Barron lived in this house on Depot Street with children Anna, Greta, and William. John held the positions of Lyme supervisor and justice of the peace and was a business leader. The house remained in the Barron family until the death of daughters Anna, a former supervisor at VanDuzee Memorial Hospital in Gouverneur, and Greta, a former teacher in the Three Mile Bay and Watertown school systems.

The Wells house stands to the right. The steeple of one of the two Baptist church towers rises in the distance. The vacant space is where the G. R. Wilcox Store once stood before it was destroyed by fire in 1887. Fires were a common occurrence in early years. Bucket brigades were the only way available to fight a fire unless a nearby town owned fire equipment. Many times a building would burn to the ground before help arrived.

Opposite the Barron Block stood the residence of Isaac C. Wells. Large, elaborate homes were built from money earned selling hay. Roomy houses allowed for social functions and guests to be housed within the home when entertaining. Wells held the positions of justice of the peace and town clerk for the Town of Lyme.

This photograph shows the street known as Wells Street before it became lined with houses. Isaac C. Wells was one of the first settlers. In 1827, Wells settled an area located about one and one half miles north of the hamlet where he erected a limestone house. This road led to the Three Mile Bay depot after which the street was renamed, Depot Street.

Farming was the occupation followed by James and Adelaide Herrick Cornaire. They lived on the Herrick homestead until 1912 and then moved to this house located on Wells Street, where they resided until 1944.

The Charles J. Rickett house was located on Wells Street. Rickett was a farmer and served in Company E of the 186th New York Infantry.

Verna and Ross Terrill ran a grocery store on Main Street. Verna was born in the town of Worth. Ross was born on March 22, 1888, in Three Mile Bay. The store closed in the mid-1960s after 32 years of operation. Favorites from the 1¢ candy collection were coconut strips and hot balls. Ross paid local residents 1¢ per night crawler or minnow so that he could supply his fishing customers with bait.

Claude Mount lived in this residence (right) on Depot Street. This is a view of the house taken from the neighboring backyard of Bill and Margaret Steverson. Margaret taught children at the union school in Three Mile Bay.

Green R. Wilcox ran a general merchandise store on Main Street. Green was the son of shipbuilder Asa Wilcox by his first marriage to Cynthia Hill. Green married Mary Antoinette, daughter of Joseph and Betsey Corey Fellows. The G. R. Wilcox Store prospered until the fire of 1887 destroyed the building along with all the stock. The store was rebuilt.

Charles McKinstry purchased the former Schuyler, McKinstry and Company and operated it as C. W. McKinstry dry goods store, as shown by this 1885 trade card. Trade cards and postcards were common ways of advertising businesses in the late 1800s and could be purchased by the retailer for $7.50 for 500, $10 for 1,000.

Ward W. Mount started his general store carrier by selling groceries at the Handy Store. A pair of boots sold for a total sum of $1.90 in 1884 in dry goods stores located in Three Mile Bay.

Store coins were often used as a form of barter. This coin was dispensed from the Ward W. Mount general store in exchange for merchandise such as eggs. It is the equivalent to the sum of 25¢.

Early general stores usually displayed products using counter space and shelving. Shown is arranged merchandise waiting to be sold at the Mount general store; displays were simple. Numerous products and numerous amounts of each product could be found on each display rack.

John B. Taylor moved the family house from Main Street to the shoreline of Three Mile Bay, where it stands today. The Taylor house was remodeled to Colonial Revival design after its move to the shores of the bay. (Courtesy of Sharon Clark.)

Dr. Waterman A. Vincent contracted for the construction of this 20-by-45-foot block with Leonard and Gilmour of Dexter. Where the building stood was known as the Lansing block. Vincent carried a general line of drugs/medicines. His store was spared during the 1887 fire.

This house, built around the 1870s, and carriage and harness shop located to the left of the Methodist church on Main Street were owned by John L. and Lonah Fox Taylor. After the death of John L., son John B. had the house moved to the shores of Three Mile Bay.

View of T.M. Bay Three Mile

State Street ran from Main Street down and along the water's edge, as shown by this photograph. When the road was redesigned, State Street was eliminated. The road made the water more accessible. Wood waiting to be cut is on the water's edge.

The Central House Hotel, built in 1855, was owned by Daniel B. Schuyler, president of Jefferson County National Bank in Watertown. This photograph of the hotel was taken in 1886. The Central House had been a stop on the stagecoach line and the Watertown-to-Cape Vincent railroad when they were operational.

Not all but most of the visitors and hamlet residents are identified here. From left to right are Walton Hall, a boy with his bike, James Ryder, William Barber, Edward Barber, Jacob Fox, George Hyatt, and Byron Mount.

⋆FAREWELL✝PARTY⋆

AT THE

Central House, Three Mile Bay,

Wednesday Evening, March 28th, 1883.

YOURSELF AND LADY ARE RESPECTFULLY INVITED.

ROOM COMMITTEE.

Eugene Fry,   Ezra Crouse,   Wm. Gaskell,   D. Ryder,   Jay Smith,
John Lingenfelter,   W. O. Whitney,   Emmet Collins,   Dr. W. A. Vincent.

Tickets, including Supper, $1.50.   **B. A. WILCOX, Proprietor.**

This 1883 formal invitation was not uncommon during the time the Central House was functional. B. A. Wilcox, along with the Room Committee, extended an invitation to guests to attend a farewell supper for the cost of $1.50.

MAIN ST. WEST. THREE MILE BAY. N. Y.

This house is of Victorian style and is shown with an outhouse that would have been used because there were few indoor bathrooms. One can see the ruins of buildings that were formerly located on the street.

The Town Tavern stood on Main Street until the Three Mile Bay Fire Department bought and tore it down to build a new fire station. A house belonging to Goldie Dick was also torn down to make way for the hall. It was common for patrons to stop and enjoy lunch or dinner in the tavern dining room. (Courtesy of Sharon Clark.)

Carriage and wagon makers were in demand. Fred, John, and Mark Barber of Three Mile Bay were boatbuilders, and Fred was also a fisherman. This is the Barber house located on Main Street.

John and Eliza Whitmore lived in the cup and saucer home at Three Mile Bay. The architectural design, built in the early 1800s, was named such for its resemblance to articles of tableware. John is shown walking toward the house. He went fishing for sunfish daily in good weather. The house no longer stands. (Courtesy of Sharon Clark.)

Two

CHURCHES AND CELEBRATIONS

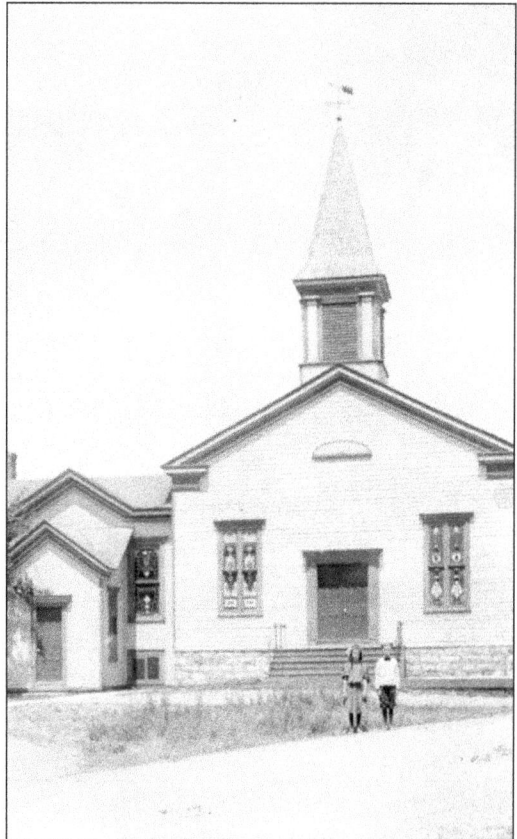

In 1838, the Baptist church at Point Salubrious disbanded and the church at Three Mile Bay took on the name First Baptist Church of Lyme. The church was completed at a cost of $2,000, in time for the December 24, 1840, service. Reverend Whitman continued preaching every other Sunday in Three Mile Bay and the remaining time between Chaumont and Indian Ridge. Marion Dick and an Irwin boy stand in front of the church. (Courtesy of Sharon Clark.)

Shown is the interior of the Baptist church in Three Mile Bay. Many of the furnishings, including the chair and table, have remained at the church and are still being used by members of the Baptist church congregation. (Courtesy of Sharon Clark.)

Youths of the Baptist Church participated in a Christmas program in 1962. Rev. Glenfield Gifford was the minister. Several in the photograph are the children of the Giffords.

Depauville resident Benjamin Dyden with committee members David and Eliza McComber, Benjamin and Abigal Manning, and Prudence Caswell formed the Three Mile Bay Episcopal Church in 1838. The church was completed in 1854 and cost $5,000. Asa Wilcox gifted the church bell and Elizabeth Main a melodeon. The church bell rang for the first time at the funeral of Byron Wilcox, son of Asa, who lost his life at the launching of a ship at the Wilcox shipyard.

A 1947 picnic is enjoyed by the Methodist Sunday school group at Long Point State Park, Point Peninsula. Sunday school groups met often. Usually there was a scheduled meeting time where the young adults met to learn and enjoy their time together.

A meeting of the Methodist youth group includes, from left to right, (first row) Grace Reed, Betty Weaver, Shirley Hoppel, Eleanor Reed, Dorothy Reed, Ruth Scales, June Brown, JoAnn West, Elsie Reed, and Aderbelt Brigman; (second row) George Parker, Jean Brill, Jim Klock, Gene Parker, Bob Daily, and Albert Klock.

Covered-dish suppers were common, and everyone would prepare their special dishes. Methodist church members, from left to right, two unidentified, Elva Jean Mount, Elaine Becker, Ginger Becker (child), and Marion Northrop meet for a covered-dish supper.

Point Peninsula, formerly Wilcoxville, has a church that has become fondly known as the "Little White Church by the Lake." Of the Methodist faith, it serves local and summer residents. The steeple of the church can be seen in the view beyond the Point Peninsula Hotel.

The 1941 participants of a Christmas program at the Point Peninsula Methodist Church, from left to right, are (first row) Harrison J. Mason; Earl VanNess; Nancy VanNess; Rex Casler; Mildred Collins; Sonny Pearson; and Mildred Countryman; (second row) Harold Russell; Joyce Barr; Marilyn Bongard; Mavis Countryman; Mrs. Paul Eddy, director; unidentified; and Dorothy Cheal, organist; (third row) Gladys VanNess; Garnett Barr; Jean Eddy; Mildred VanNess; Florence VanNess; Virginia Eddy; Nancy Pearson; and Barbara Eddy; (fourth row) Carl Russell; unknown; Paul Southwell; John Henry Failing; Robert Gillette; David Blandon; and Ervin Barr. (Courtesy of the Watertown Daily Times.)

A wedding shower was held for Anna Merz on October 6, 1947. Shown from left to right are Thelma Ross, Charlotte Nichols, Marion Yott, Jeannine Narrigan, and Anna Merz.

Doris B. Gonseth, nurse at Lyme Central, was honored at a wedding reception that took place on May 12, 1948, in Three Mile Bay. From left to right are Marilyn Bourcy, Edna Bourcy, unidentified, Mabel Herrick, Doris Gonseth, unidentified, and Myrtle Wilcox.

Anna Merz (right) and Mrs. William Harding are shown at a shower in 1947 prior to Merz's marriage to Earl Jackson. Before her wedding ceremony, Frank Cheal sang "I Love You Truly" and "Always" with accompaniment by Anna Barron, who also played the wedding march. They were married on a Saturday at 8:00 p.m. at the Methodist church at Three Mile Bay, on October 11, 1947.

Shown at the Mount house are, from left to right, Shirley Cobb, the bride Corabelle "Corky" Cobb, the groom Spencer Mount, and Richard Mount. This photograph was taken the day of the wedding between Spencer and Corky, July 16, 1950.

The wedding of Ola Yott and Vernon Mitchell took place on August 7, 1949. Ola wore a traditional white satin gown fashioned with a lace bodice skirt that ended in a lace-trimmed train. She wore a fingertip veil and carried a white prayer book and roses. From left to right, Howard Yott, Clinton Mitchell, Vernon and Ola, Marion Yott, and Mildred Mitchell pose for the camera.

Abertina (left) Becker and Ivan Becker are shown celebrating their 50th wedding anniversary in 1967. From left to right, daughter Marilyn Crouse, Kathy Crouse, and daughter Joan Salenski also join in the celebration.

Clarence "Ox" Holbrook and Barbara Luff were married on August 24, 1952, at the Little White Church, Point Peninsula. Barbara delivered the rural mail on Point Peninsula.

Ben Countryman (left) attended the wedding of his daughter Lois Countryman with daughter Mavis Countryman and granddaughter Wendy Hubbard. The Countryman family resided on Point Peninsula.

The wedding of Lois Countryman and Chuck Brownell took place at Three Mile Bay. The couple is shown at the Town Tavern Hotel. Through the years that the tavern has been open, owners of the establishment have changed. Stan Percy and Harlow and Vera Fitzgerald were previous owners.

Ruth Weiler, a former Three Mile Bay resident, was wed in a ceremony on March 25, 1960, at Massena to Wallace (Wally) Hunter.

From left to right, Faye Garrett, Cathie Garret, and Hazel Davis attend a wedding shower for Cathie at the home of Mary Klock. Jim Davis and Cathie were married at All Saints Church, Chaumont, on July 19, 1969.

Claude and Blanche Rickett congratulate groom William Matice and bride Kathy Holbrook Matice on June 30, 1973, at the Point Peninsula Church. Marion Pickett greets Julie Holbrook; the young woman on the right is unidentified.

The Bachelor Cemetery, the first cemetery of Three Mile Bay, was located along Lott's Cove, Three Mile Point. The limestone makeup of the terrain made it difficult to properly bury residents. In many areas, the gravestones of early cemeteries have been removed and used for construction purposes. Wrought iron fences that adorned and guarded the cemeteries of the dead have also been removed.

The Three Mile Bay Cemetery was relocated to the west side in the hamlet. This is a side view of the area. The vault that is located in the cemetery is constructed of marble mined from Gouverneur. Mrs. George Potter, wife of a former dentist from Cape Vincent, raised the $2,300 needed to complete the construction of the vault. (Courtesy of Sharon Clark.)

Three

SCHOOLS

The union school built in 1878 in the hamlet was referred to as District No. 5. The school was centralized into the Lyme district in 1942. Classes were broken up into one section of fourth, fifth, and sixth grades with another section made up of first, second, and third grades. Clarence Daley (son of Morris Daley) and Bessie Shaw are shown standing in front of the school in this early photograph. (Courtesy of Sharon Clark.)

This photograph of the Wells Settlement School house and children is dated 1914. Shown from left to right are (first row) Irene Wells, George Cummings, Clarence Rickett, Spencer Shaw, Frances Fleury, Doris Cranston, and Claude Rickett; (second row) Martha Cranston, unidentified, Anna Fleury, and Bill Constance; (third row) Ross Wells, Lyman Craston, Floyd Clark, Mildred Fleury, Lavilla Chavoustie, Margaret Fleury, Hazel Constance, and Emerance Eselin.

This photograph of classmates with their teacher and Reverend Nichols (back row, second from right) was taken at the Three Mile Bay Union School. Identification of the students is not available, nor is the date of the photograph. Many older photographs will never be identified. It is not always the practice to write the identification of each person. This is what has happened to this photograph.

Shown in this 1917 photograph is teacher Florence Beadle at Three Mile Bay Union School. Classes at the union school were taught by teachers who had once been students at the school. It was not uncommon for teachers to work for short periods of time as Beadle did. Heads of early schools did not approve of pregnant women teaching.

This photograph is of (from left to right) Eva Cross, Iva Bates, and Irene Wells standing in front of the entrance to the union school, Three Mile Bay.

Mabel Herrick began her teaching career at the one-room schoolhouse on Point Peninsula with five students. She lived in Glen Park and traveled by streetcar to Brownville, by train from Brownville to Three Mile Bay, and completed the remaining 22 miles to Point Peninsula by wagon before arriving at the school in a horse and buggy. Her wages for her first year of teaching were $320. Mabel and Claude Herrick resided in the bay for over 45 years.

Myrtle Wilcox Nicholson taught for 26 years at the Three Mile Bay Union School. She also taught at the Fox Creek District. Nicholson traveled to Europe in July and August 1953 in preparation for taking her masters, which she obtained in 1954. Nicholson retired when the school closed in 1968. (Courtesy of Gary and Sharon Nicholson.)

Shown is the 1905 football team of the Three Mile Bay High School. From left to right are (first row) Glen Lance, unidentified, Luke Salsbury, Van Wilcox, and Percy Cosselman; (second row) Perl Vosler, Lloyd Watkins, Will Northrop, Glen Watkins, George Dick, and Roy Northrop; (third row) principal ? Bennett, Ray Northrop, Henry Northrop, unidentified, and Rev. Frank Andre of the Methodist Church.

This Three Mile Bay Union School group of first, second, third, and fourth graders was taken in 1920. Identified from left to right are (first row) Dorothy Miller, Doris Butler, Anna Rogers, Mary Whattam, Beulah Hamilton, and Nellie Bretch, teacher; (second row) Clarence Herrick, Henry Herrick, John Butler, and Morris Plato. (Courtesy of Betsy and Ed Herrick.)

Children attending combined grades in early elementary schools were of different age groups, and sisters and brothers could even be in the same classroom. Shown from left to right are (first row) Audrey Yott, Judy Chavoustie, Sherry Bourcy, and Janice Yott; (second row) Carolyn Herrick, Elaine Northrop, Mary Ann Muckelwee, Sue Bourcy, and Mary Yott.

Janice Yott, left, and Dianne Thompson attend a function at the union school. Christmas programs and other special holiday programs were put on at the school. During the special Christmas programs, small boxed candy would be handed out and the children would receive a visit from Santa.

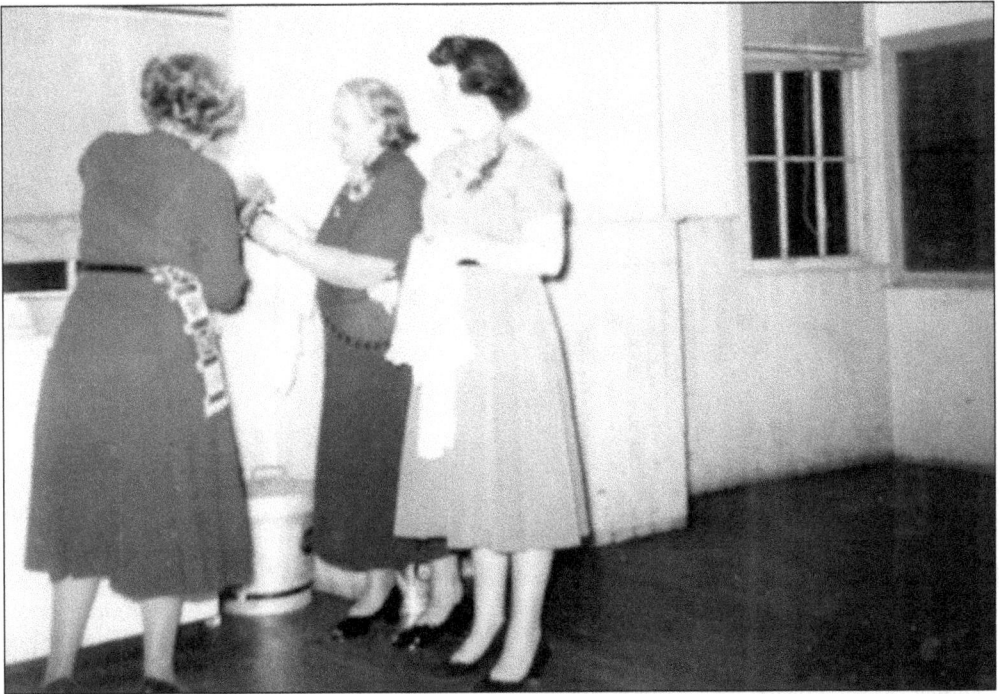

Mary Northrop Klock, center, and two unidentified women are shown cleaning up after a special function at the union school in Three Mile Bay. Food was usually prepared by community residents.

Reul (left) and Brad Gifford, sons of Rev. and Mrs. Glenfield Gifford, are shown playing on the swing set at the elementary school in Three Mile Bay. The playground was accessible and utilized by children of the hamlet during and after school hours.

Shown is a 1950s group picture taken of students attending the Three Mile Bay Union School. From left to right are (first row) Janice Yott, Diane Comins, Cindy Phillips, and Judy Chavoustie; (second row) Sheri Bourcy, Jennifer Ross, Audrey Yott, Janice Luff, Alice Whitmore, Sally Reddick, Mary Rogers, and Georganna Rogers; (third row) Brad Gifford, David Seymour, Donnie Goutremont, David Krause, Dick Schrieber, Hubert Seymour, and Paul Klock; (fourth row) Mabel Herrick, teacher.

Mabel Herrick (first row, right) is shown at a Parent-Teacher Association gathering in celebration of 33 years of teaching. With Herrick are, from left to right, (first row) Mildred Harris; (second row) Milford Collins, Wilford Kilburn, Judson Kilburn, and Harley Dingman, the first five students she taught at the one-room schoolhouse on Point Peninsula.

This 1967 photograph shows students attending the union school. The ground floor was used to teach students in grades one through three. The upstairs floor of the building housed the students in grades four through six.

Enjoying a meal at the school in June 1968 are Reba Yott in the center in the back, Corky Mount on the far right in the back, and Agnes Bedoar in the right foreground. Functions such as this were usually attended by a large number of residents from the area. There was a small kitchen in the school that was utilized when special functions were held in the school building.

Sigrid Utess and Rev. Glenfield Gifford of the Baptist Church also attended the June function. The school officially closed its doors on July 1, 1968.

Shown in the background is the new brick Chaumont High School, which was built in 1938. With the closing of Three Mile Bay Union School, all district students attended the high school at Chaumont.

Shown in this Lyme basketball photograph from left to right are (first row) Albert Klock, George Larabee, Bill Hewitt, Dick Warner, Phil McAdam, Paul Gosier, and coach Hartz; (second row) Dick Steverson, Sonny Salvatore, Albert "Pete" Krause, Frank Winslow, and Albert "Bud" Young.

The Lyme Central School marching band participated at regional celebrations. Shown from left to right are the Lyme majorettes (first row) Sandra Mumford, Rita Hewitt, Donna Mumford, and Ann Chavoustie; (second row) Lois Quencer, Janet Heinz, Donna Brown, and Joseph Collins, band instructor.

The 1952 Lyme baseball team from left to right includes (first row) T. Goodale, W. Gosier, William Cuppernell, Larry Comins, J. Gosier, and Jim West; (second row) R. Purcell, J. Fulmer, Donnie Rickett, JoAnn West, coach William West, Tommy Dunham, Noel Prior, and Harvey Hewitt; (third row) Guy Gosier, Marty Bancroft, Jim Kock, V. Weaver, J. Becker, and Maurice Peters.

Parked beside Lyme Central School are the buses that were used during the 1950s. Before school transportation, children would walk to school, sometimes for miles.

Cheerleaders supported the school and their team. Shown from left to right are Elinor Merchant, Beverly Greenizan, Margaret Failing, Mary Lou Wilkenson, Beverly Wilkenson, Evelyn Crump, Pat Klock, and Edith Warner.

These Lyme Central School students are Joanne Bourne (left) and Christine Becker. Both attended Lyme Central School at Chaumont. Children and young adults from Three Mile Bay attended the school after Three Mile Bay Union School closed its doors in 1968.

Lois Quencer (first row, left), Barbara Mason (first row, right), Susie Purcell (second row, left), and Barbara Bower (second row, right) are show together at the Chaumont High School. Scarves and sashes were the fashion of this time period.

A 1950s play is held in the gymnasium at the high school in Chaumont. Each school year, students would participate in the production of a school-supervised play. Auditions would be given, and the person whose performance appeared to be exceptional would be cast for one of the leads, and others would be placed accordingly.

Four

EARLY AGRICULTURE AND CHEESE MAKING

Farmers occupied much of the land. Shown is Ken Lance with a sleigh. In the background, the Fox farm can be seen. In later years, this site would house a restaurant, Earl Jackson's marine and auto repair shop, homes, and cottages. (Courtesy of Don Lance.)

Hiram and Chasine Huntley Herrick moved to this Ashland Road farm after their July 19, 1835, wedding. Chasine came from Vermont by ox team to Herkimer about 1830. She taught school before moving to Three Mile Bay.

This farm, the original Charles and Helen Beamus Rickett homestead, is located on McCombs Settlement Road in Chaumont. Owners did not always farm the land themselves. A hired hand was employed and lived directly on the farm.

This upright hay press was used to transfer cut hay into the mow of a barn. The men on the platform are called jumpers. Several farmers in the area owned hay presses, including Ralph Reed, Ted Klock, and Phillip Merchant. Andrew Whattam often assisted those working on the threshing.

This is an early machine that was used to thresh. An Oliver binder was used to bind the wheat ahead of the threshing machine in the 1940s. Early Quakers threshed crops with old-time flails, working by hand to thresh grain on the barn floors. Horses were even used to trample out the grain.

Tractors were not obtainable in early farming. When models came out on the market, they were very expensive. Many could not or did not want to pay an extreme price for a farming product. The furrows of hay can be seen. Team horses were used in early farm life to do many of the heavy chores.

Perl Phelps plowed his fields using a team of horses. He takes a moment to hold his dog Teddy. Farmers usually removed pieces of limestone from farmland that they were going to plow. They used the stones to form a fence around the perimeter of their fields.

Don and Ken Lance are shown on Point Peninsula loading the barn after the threshing was completed. Modern threshing machines draw the grain down and through the many teeth, which are set below the cylinder. What are known as pioneer machines operate with the cylinder turning in the opposite direction and draw the grain up and through the threshing teeth set above and the straw and chaff fall on the threshing machine floor. The old threshing cylinder was larger, and the teeth in the cylinder were like large staples. The newly built barn is typical of the structures designed during the 1940s. Many barns of this time period have been conserved through "red barn" grants.

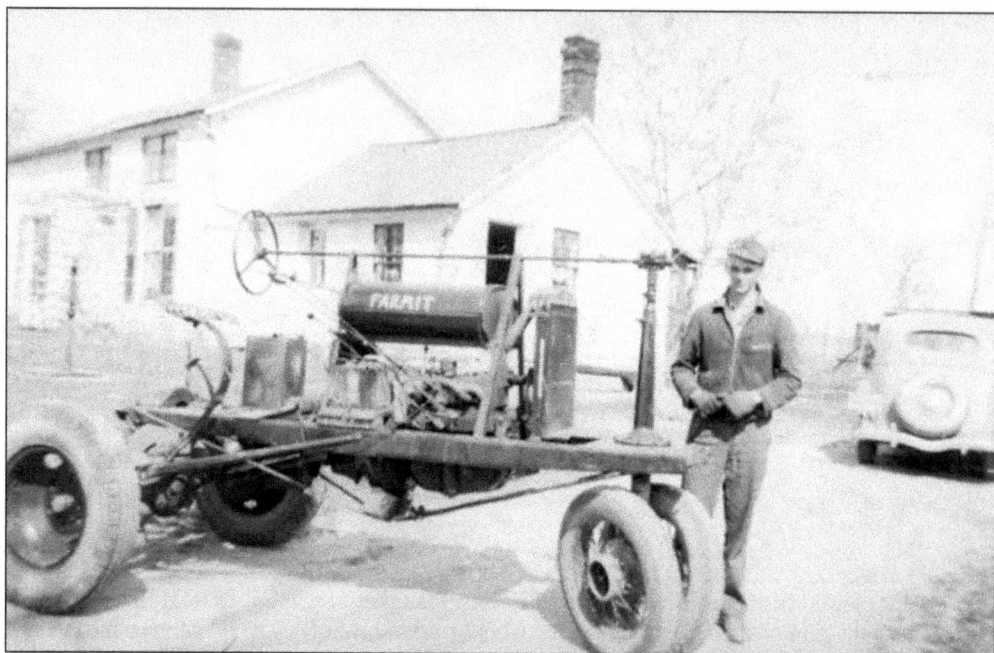

Ken Lance visited his uncle Richard Merchant on the Valley Road and soon found that he had a great interest in International tractors. In 1938, he made a "farmit" tractor from a Model A frame, an engine, and two transmissions. The tractor worked well and was used daily to do chores, including mowing. The following year Ken Lance purchased an International Farmall H for $800. (Courtesy of Don Lance.)

Several owners went from farm to farm using their threshing machines to do chores for those who did not have the equipment to do their farmwork. H. G. is shown threshing.

Horses were used for farming, and they were used for riding enjoyment. Doris W. Graves can be seen riding a pony on a farm at Three Mile Bay. There was a time when every household kept a horse or horses to perform numerous chores around the farm.

Farming was one of the first trades carried on by people in rural areas. In the 1800s, a farmer would be considered a farmer whether they owned 2 or 20 head of livestock. A rural community intermingles, as can be seen by the cows grazing on one side of the bay while a boat and men stand on the opposite bank along the line of the hamlet.

Clarence Rickett used his pony to herd cattle. Clarence's father, Brighton Rickett, a former county deputy sheriff and constable, and mother stand in the background.

Caroline, Ronnie, and Eddie Herrick are shown at Chaumont with a surrey that originally came from the Fox farm located at the top of the hill in Three Mile Bay. (Courtesy of Betsy and Ed Herrick.)

Shown are farmers with their milk wagons in 1912 in front of the general store. It was an impressive sight as the wagons traveled down Main Street on their way to and returning from delivering their milk to the creamery/cheese factory. (Courtesy of Sharon Clark.)

Sitting along the shoreline of Three Mile Bay behind the Three Mile Bay cheese plant is Asher Corse, cheese maker. J. Taft was the owner/manager in Three Mile Bay. David and Claude Mount purchased a cheese plant in Three Mile Bay in 1915 and sold it to E. N. Coon in 1920.

The creamery was located on the shores of Three Mile Bay. Local farmers delivered their products by horse and wagon. A ledger book dated January 18, 1909, lists a total of $41.51 paid to the cheese factory for purchases for resale at the local general store. (Courtesy of Sharon Clark.)

Shown is a full side view of the cheese factory. The process of cheese making was brought from England by early settlers. Cheese making was mainly done at home for a family's personal use. The process was expensive, and soon it was realized that making cheese on a larger scale would be less expensive. (Courtesy of Sharon Clark.)

Five

FISHING AND THE BUILDING OF A RAILROAD

R. W. & O. TRAIN AT ROME STATION, 1878

The train of the Rome, Watertown and Ogdensburg Railroad (RW&O) sits at the Rome station. The train traveled the tracks from Rome to Watertown and beyond. The rails for the Cape Vincent branch extension reached Chaumont on November 20, 1851, and surpassed the depot of Three Mile Bay, one mile north of the hamlet, in April 1852. (Courtesy of George Cataldo.)

73

Shown is the first depot built at Three Mile Bay. The mail wagon next to the building belonged to William Bates. Bates carried mail, drove a passenger bus to and from the depot, and was a local farmer. The depot was located one mile from any civilization. Passengers embarking on the train had to have a means of reaching their final destination. Many arrived to participate in the sport of fishing, while salesmen frequented local stores to take orders. (Courtesy of Sharon Clark.)

The remains of the first depot at Three Mile Bay are shown after fire destroyed it in 1917. The New York Central Railroad station caught fire at 1:00 p.m. The fire is believed to have been caused by sparks from a passing train. Train accidents sometimes did happen and caused considerable damage. (Courtesy of Don Lance.)

Dr. John and Marion Dick stand beside the second train depot built at Three Mile Bay on August 31, 1926. Originally the RW&O, the line was incorporated into the New York Central in 1914. (Courtesy of Jeannine Narrigan.)

In winter, snow had to be cleared from the tracks running from Watertown to Cape Vincent. This 1927/1928 photograph shows an early snowplow parked down by the old depot in Watertown. (Courtesy of Don Lance.)

Limestone was durable. Kyle Grant and his dog Cookie stand beneath this trestle that is made of limestone quarried from the land where it is constructed. After the demise of the rail, farmers used the bed of the old railroad line to herd their cows from one farm to pasture in neighboring fields. (Courtesy of Paul Norton.)

Perl Vosler (right) is shown with an unidentified person displaying their black bass limit catch of 12. (Courtesy of Sharon Clark.)

Fishermen Perl Vosler (left) and an unidentified person pose with a lake sturgeon that was caught in one of Vosler's netting excursions. The fish was so large that a rope was attached to a fin and it was towed by boat back to shore. Ted Utess, as a young boy, helped to load the nine-foot fish onto a truck for the trip to Vosler's shanty. (Courtesy of Sharon Clark.)

Many people of the area were fishermen. Fishing was profitable, and markets in New York City, Albany, and beyond were made obtainable because of the railroad. Clarence Cheal, a fisherman, is shown with a 154-pound lake sturgeon caught by Simon P. Failing. (Courtesy of Sharon Clark.)

Gill nets were used for fishing. Nets were laid out to dry on the rocks and were repaired in the Mount general store on the second floor where there was plenty of room to spread the nets out. The gill of a fish would become entangled with the net and would have to be removed manually. (Courtesy of Sharon Clark.)

John Lance and his wife, Georgia Merchant Lance, farmed the Fox homestead on Three Mile Point before moving to the Milton Lance farm in 1921. John also worked as a commercial fisherman, making most of his own nets, and continued fishing as a hobby after his retirement from farming. John Lance's fishing shanty in May 1927 could be identified by the sturgeon head attached to its side. (Courtesy of Don Lance.)

The 1927 license plate identifies the year that fisherman John Lance drove his Model T up the hill on his way to deliver the day's catch of fish to the train depot. A blooming crab apple tree looms over Don Lance, age seven, who sits on the wooden boxes filled with fish that soon would be salted, packed in ice, and transferred to barrels lined with sawdust before being placed on the train headed for markets in New York City. (Courtesy of Don Lance.)

Boats moored in Bellinger's Cove between 1910 and 1915 belonged to John Lance and Merton Huck. The very warm summer day called for a quick swim by those traveling in the boats. There are many coves situated along the shoreline. Summer cottages and even year-round residences line the shores of Three Mile Bay. (Courtesy of Don Lance.)

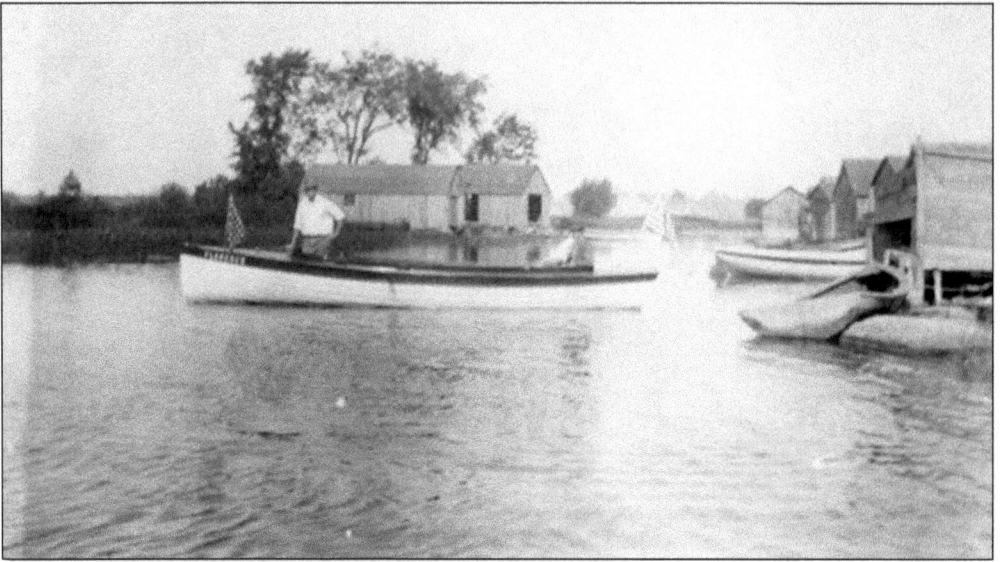

Boating was used to make a financial profit and was also a favorite pastime of residents, summer and year-round, as shown here by the boat *Florence*. (Courtesy of Sharon Clark.)

The tranquility of area waters beckoned those living on or near the bay to enjoy it. Shown is an unidentified woman with her dog. St. Lawrence skiffs and canoes were popular. Today they are a collector's item. Three Mile Bay was much deeper in the early years.

Six

WATERWAYS AND POINTS

This is the view that boaters saw when sailing on Three Mile Bay. On the horizon are fishing shanties to the right, the sawmill that was built in 1820 by Peter and Richard Estes at the mouth of Three Mile Creek is in the center, and the shore of the bay where the shipyard of Asa Wilcox once was located is on the left. (Courtesy of Sharon Clark.)

The sawmill of Peter and Richard Estes was built of wood and native limestone blocks. The limestone ruins can be seen along the edge of Three Mile Creek. In 1860, Menzo Wheeler purchased and rebuilt the mill.

A gas engine helped to produce waterpower harnessed from Three Mile Creek. The mill had the capacity to produce 500,000 feet of lumber annually. Native limestone can be seen in the construction of the mill.

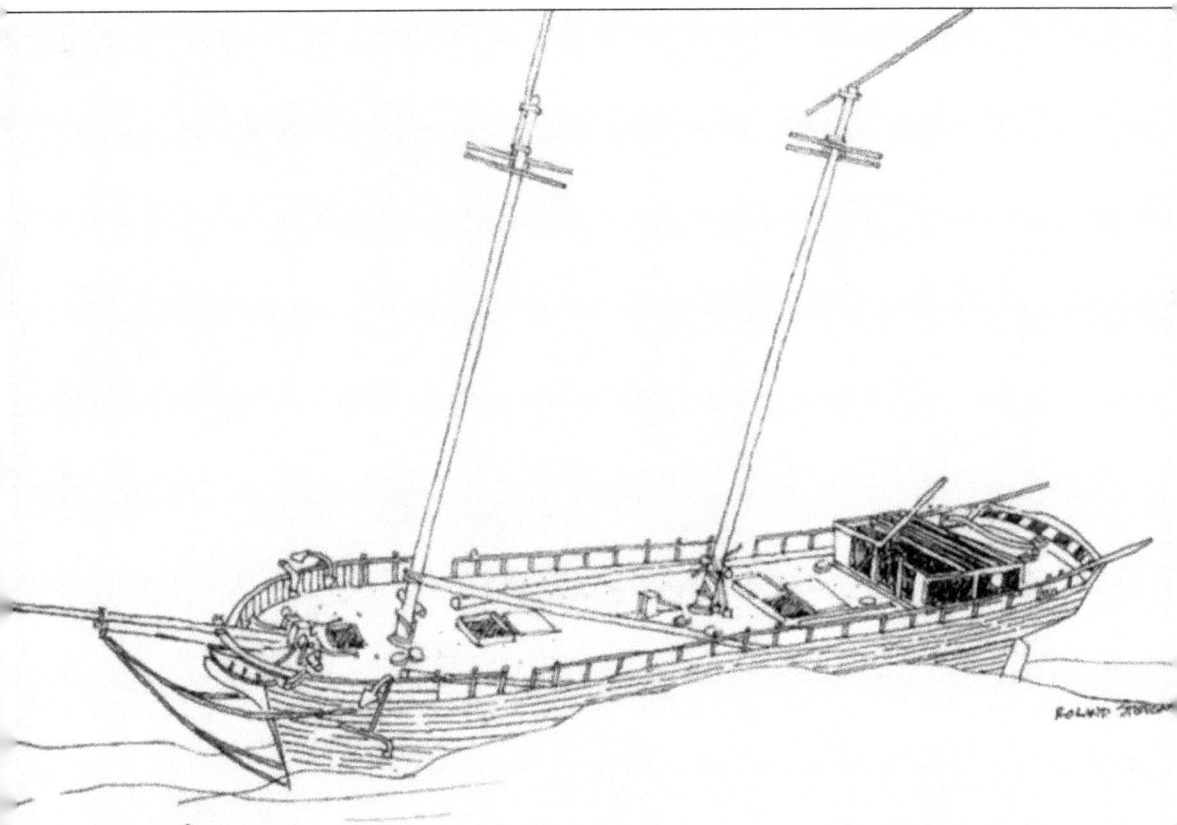

Asa Wilcox was both a blacksmith and a boatbuilder by trade. He was also one of the first founders of Three Mile Bay. He became know as a master shipbuilder as he created a total of 48 sailing vessels. In 1845, he built the *Milan*, a 147-ton schooner, at his shipyard at Three Mile Bay. Through the years many shipwrecks have been discovered. This wreck was discovered by divers Jim Kennard and Dan Scoville. (Courtesy of Chip Stevens.)

This limestone house, reminiscent of early native limestone architecture of Jefferson County, is located on the North Shore Road overlooking Chaumont Bay. Built in 1838 for Charles M. Wilcox, the house and property remained in the Wilcox family until the death of Mabel Wilcox Nicholson, a former Three Mile Bay Union School teacher.

The Carrying Place at the Isthmus was frequented by Native Americans, the Iroquois, who carried their canoes across the isthmus, which connects Point Peninsula with land. It has always been a tradition that young adults from the area camp on the isthmus during summer months. This is Lester Angell, with dog Pal, cooking over a campfire during his stay in August 1922.

During the 1950s, Gladys and Wilson Southwell ran a restaurant in the former Earl Cooley store located in the summer resort of Point Peninsula. Gladys was well known in the restaurant business because of her ability to serve a good meal. (Courtesy of Sharon Clark.)

Shown is the interior of the establishment that the Southwells operated. Booths and small tables were available for customers to enjoy their meals. (Courtesy of Sharon Clark.)

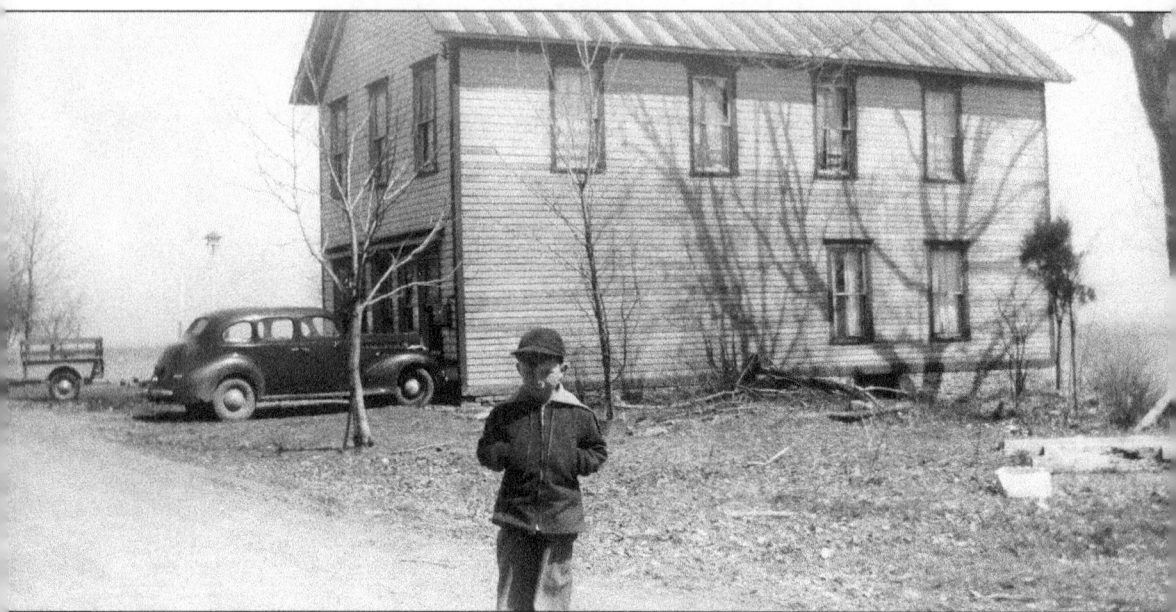

Shown in 1950 is Fred Southwell, son of Wilson and Gladys Southwell, standing in front of the Grange hall, which was constructed from lumber taken from a Point Peninsula dock. The Independent Order of Old Fellows used the Grange building until 1959. (Courtesy of Sharon Clark.)

Iceboat races were popular in the 1930s. Shown preparing for a day of racing are Ken and Don Lance (front, left), Delos Hagen and Meade Hayes in the boats (front right), and John Hewitt (back, center) on the ice on Three Mile Bay. Both the hamlet and Three Mile Point can be seen in the distance. This was a time period when people could be seen enjoying the cold and snow during winter weather months. (Courtesy of Don Lance.)

Shown in 1927 from left to right are John Ahlheim, Norm Ahlheim, and Norman Ahlheim wearing swimsuits of the time period.

The shore is lined with summer cottages. On the far right is the Ahlheim residence located on Three Mile Point. The cottage at one time had been an old garage. The Ahlheim family refurbished the building. (Courtesy of John Ahlheim.)

Lott's Cove is the location where the stone from the limestone quarry would be loaded for transport by waterway. The first cemetery for the hamlet of Three Mile Bay was also located at Lott's Cove on Three Mile Bay.

Butter Milk Falls, named for its buttermilk appearance, is located on the Chaumont–Depauville Road in Chaumont.

John Barron owned a limestone quarry on Three Mile Point. Working with stone was labor intensive. Blocks were loaded onto barges using block and tackle, manpower, and horses. John B. Taylor was responsible for Barron supplying limestone for many elaborate buildings such as the Paddock Arcade and the House of the Good Samaritan Hospital, Watertown. (Courtesy of the Watertown Daily Times.)

Large blocks of limestone from this quarry owned by J. Schuyler Fox and operated by Adams and Fish of Chaumont, located on Three Mile Point, were used to build the Barge Canal locks in 1922. The federal government made purchases of limestone from the Fox farm from 1860 to 1870. (Courtesy of the Watertown Daily Times.)

Perl Phelps was a Great Lakes and St. Lawrence River captain. He sailed under the flags of Eldridge and Robinson Company, Fulton; Captain Hinkley Company, Oswego; and Adams and Duforth Company, Chaumont. Upon his retirement, he partnered with his brother Frank and built the sailing schooner *Emma* and steamers *John S. Parson, Frank Phelps,* and *M. G. Phelps.*

This limestone structure was the office of Adams and Duford Company, which, along with several other firms, represented the interest of limestone in the Chaumont area. It operated two kilns and oversaw the workings of several of the area quarries.

The draw gate, located in Chaumont, is open to let the ship carrying limestone pass. A captain of a ship, such as Perl Phelps, would have a license to carry hay or limestone from the breakwater to the peninsula.

This was the Salubrious Club House, located on Point Salubrious, Chaumont. An elaborate club set on the shores of Lake Ontario, the 10-acre property originally attracted visitors because of a sulfur spring located on the property. The club charged member dues but was never a profitable venture. In 1914, W. H. Moore gave a one-year use to Trinity Church, later donating the property to the church in 1915. The church eventually disposed of the property valued at $15,999.

In 1914–1915, iceboat racing and skate sailing were popular pastime sports on local area waters. The ice had to be in pristine shape and free of snow for the white-sailed boats to skim freely over the ice. The runners on the skates "hummed and scraped" as operators whizzed across the ice. Competition between villages was common. In February 1938, iceboat racing was again enacted. Harry Gould's boat of Three Mile Bay won one of the four races in a competition between Chaumont and Watertown. Other entrants competing were Mead Hayes and Ernest Gould, of Three Mile Bay. Hayes was noted for being an unbeatable iceboater but, on February 22, was defeated by skipper Earle Taber, of Watertown, who won two of the four races.

On Three Mile Point are numerous summer cottages. In 1887, located at the cottage on the right, were carriage makers from Watertown fishing for the day. The area was well known for the fish that came from the bays.

Seven

THE FIRE DEPARTMENT AND ORGANIZATIONS

It was not uncommon for small hamlets and villages to not have their own operational fire departments. Bucket brigades had been the only way to control fires until those with the proper equipment arrived. The first building used to house the fire equipment was the leather and carriage shop of J. L. Taylor. In 1969, Thomas Belcher was the highest of three bidders and obtained ownership rights to the building, which he razed. Shown in the photograph is the first fire department building and the Belcher home.

This 1941 Chevrolet was the first truck purchased and housed in the Three Mile Bay Fire Company building. A reception was held on Wednesday, April 28, 1962, and a new 750-gallon pumper was dedicated in honor of the first fire chief of 1947, the late Earl Jackson.

This photograph shows the first squad car owned by the Three Mile Bay Fire Company. Shown in the photograph are Claude Herrick (left) and Jack Phillips. Phillips has served in the capacity of volunteer to the fire department for over 60 years. He presently holds the position of treasurer.

A Fourth of July celebration was held yearly. Prizes were awarded for best appearing fire department, fire department with the most men participating, best decorated float, best decorated bicycle, and best decorated automobile. Shown at the front left of what became known as the "kiddie parade" is Rosemary Klock.

Neighboring fire departments also participated in the July freedom celebration at the Three Mile Bay hamlet. Shown is a Chaumont fire truck. Viewers came from miles around to view the parades and participate in the festivities.

A float depicting Ken Bourcy's blue Sunoco station was good advertising for his business. Local businesses made a practice of participating in some way, if not by entering a float, by supporting with a donation or prize.

Cape Vincent was a participator in many events with its No. 1 John C. Londraville Post 832 vehicle. There was a time when a parade was held every weekend through the summer months. Villages and towns, or in this case hamlets, would take turns.

Shown is a memorial honoring individuals from the town of Lyme. In the background is the Chaumont railroad depot, which was destroyed by fire. The photograph is dated Memorial Day, 1947.

On May 4, 1969, William Utess was chief when the new fire hall to house the Three Mile Bay Fire Company was dedicated. Larry Stumpf, with a committee of Richard Schreiber, George Bourquin, Thomas Belcher Jr., and Milford Hyde, canvassed for and raised enough funds needed to build the hall. The ladies auxiliary, organized in 1950, kept the total cost down to $35,000, with a total $18,000 debt, by earning funds for the new electric kitchen. Magic shows by Ed Hayn, auxiliary-led dinners, raffles, pledges, and donations helped to fund the hall without any need for state or federal government money. An ambulance service staffed by volunteers was enacted in 1952.

A photograph of the Masons includes, from left to right, (first row) unidentified, George Rogers, Larry Reome, and Fortas Rogers; (second row) unidentified, Cliff Bongard, Les Daniels, and unidentified. Daniels owned and operated the Township Telephone Company for many years.

The Masons are shown at the Grange hall, from left to right are (first row) George Rogers, Larry Reome, Malcom Ryder, Wes Daniels, and George Emerich. The two men in the second row are unidentified. Lodge No. 172 Free and Accepted Masons was formed in 1850 with 11 charter members.

The Order of the Eastern Stars, No. 225, was formed on July 31, 1901. Shown from left to right are (first row) Mary Lou Wilkenson, Mr. and Mrs. Ben Mitchell, Alfreda Utess, Kathleen Comins, Walter Cuppernell, and three unidentified; (second row) Bessy Byam, Elnora Phillips, unidentified, Audrey Bourn, Evelyn Hawekar, and Margaret Cuppernell; (third row) two unidentified, Louise Hewitt, two unidentified, and Jane Failing; (third row) two unidentified, Marion Clapsaddle, unidentified, Blanche Rickett, and unidentified.

Participants of this August 1908 Three Mile Bay baseball team are, from left to right, (first row) George Dick, Lenard Vincent, Henry Northrop, and Roy Fairman; (second row) Will Sheldon, Perl Vosler, Fred Labdell, Ward W. Mount, Ray Hamilton, Percy Lance, and Charles Parker. From as early as the 1800s, village teams met to play one of the most popular sports of the time period, baseball. (Courtesy of Sharon Clark.)

William Cuppernell (left), Philip White (dressed in the baseball uniform), and Elizabeth White (sitting, second from right) all sit in the sandpit watching the game at Three Mile Bay.

Old-timers versus Three Mile Bay games were frequently held. The old-timers consisted of men from Clayton, Chaumont, and Three Mile Bay. Up to bat is Dick Steverson, who also played for the Red and Black football team in Watertown in 1969.

Eight

EARLY AREA DISASTERS

The 1876 seed house of Austin and Everett Rogers was located next to the train depot on Main Street in Chaumont. In 1908, the business closed and moved west. Charles Arnold ran the mill until 1919, when H. Maxfield (Max) Torrey bought the business. Named the Crescent Milling Company, it was destroyed by fire on October 15, 1949. The five-story mill building housed offices, a woodworking shop on the first floor, and the gristmill was located in the extreme rear.

A house belonging to the Martins in Chaumont caught fire and burned fiercely. The Martins had many people to help remove the belongings from their home. In the 1940s, people still did not have the equipment that was needed to fight a fire.

The surprising floods in July 1935 caused destruction. Three Mile Bay rose to a dangerous height during the two consecutive rainstorms. The boathouse located behind the Taylor mansion shows the extent to which the water rose.

The first lift bridge that was built in 1911 and spanned across Chaumont Bay was flooded after the storm of 1935. The bridge was replaced in 1958 with a steel beam bridge at a cost of approximately $490,000.

A five-day snowstorm in March 1947 made it necessary for two Piper Cubs to form a shuttle for transport between Three Mile Bay and Point Peninsula. George Rogers, flight instructor at the Northern Air Service, flew the firm's Cub, making 18 trips to Point Peninsula to collect 36 cans of milk. Shown also is John Lance. (Courtesy of Don Lance.)

Located on the ice in front of the Ward W. Mount store is Don Lance (left) with his airplane, a village kid, and his brother Failing. Marvin Northrop took the photograph. (Courtesy of Don Lance.)

From left to right, Ken Lance, Don Lance, Howard Bates, and Joyce Lance, an author and resident of Point Peninsula, used Howard Bates's Cub and Don Lance's plane, located by the hangar, to deliver needed supplies to residents stranded on Point Peninsula. The snowstorm of 1947 deposited 40 inches of snow on the area, and roads were impassable. (Courtesy of Don Lance.)

This car finally made its way from the point after the roads had been cleared of snow. In the Point Peninsula area, snow seems to accumulate to a much deeper depth than other areas. There are residents who do live year-round on the point, but they are prepared in advance with enough supplies in case they cannot drive off the point by way of the isthmus. (Courtesy of Sharon Clark.)

Nine

PEOPLE OF THE COMMUNITY

The wives of the early prominent businessmen of Three Mile Bay gathered together for this early photograph. From left to right they are (first row) Mrs. Oscar Hentz; Elsa Southwell, wife of L. W. Southwell; Louise Reasoner, wife of George Reasoner; Keziah Flanders, wife of Christopher Flanders; Mrs. Jacob Fox; and Louise Hayes, wife of Menzo Hayes; (second row) Mary Mount, wife of David Mount; Jennie Hamilton, wife of Hiriam Hamilton; Addie Hamilton, wife of Martin Hamilton; Julia Hyatt, wife of George Hyatt; Mrs. George Van Ostrand; and Eleanor Northrop, wife of John Northrop.

George Henry Klock I and his wife, Hanna, dressed their daughter Georgeanna in her finest for the camera.

Residents of Three Mile Bay gather for a social gathering on a warm summer day. There was a time when everyone dressed for the occasion. This photograph depicts some of the earlier residents of the area, but at this writing the individual people could not be identified.

Byron W. Mount, born in 1850, is shown in this early photograph. He followed the profession of house painter and in his youth was a Great Lakes sailor. Byron married Mary Elizabeth Hanson Mount on August 16, 1876.

From left to right, Adelaide Herrick Cornaire and James Cornaire, with daughter Zaidee, in dress of the early 1900s, pose for the camera of William Dick, Three Mile Bay photographer and crayon and india ink artist. Adelaide was the daughter of early pioneers Hiram and Chasine Huntley Herrick, who came to the area in 1830. Daughter Zaidee died on October 20, 1919.

Perl Vosler served in the 311 Infantry Regiment of the 78th Division in France during World War I. After he was discharged from his military duties in July 1919, he returned to Three Mile Bay, where he fished commercially. Many remember family members boating or driving to his place of business to purchase fish products. (Courtesy of Sharon Clark.)

Josephine Vosler, seen here on March 27, 1909, was the wife of Perl Vosler. (Courtesy of Sharon Clark.)

Jessie Vosler, shown on March 27, 1909, is the daughter of Perl and Josephine Vosler. (Courtesy of Sharon Clark.)

Shown are Earl and Viola Klock, children of Thomas Cady and Edith Fredenburg Klock. It was not uncommon during the early 1900s for adults and children to have their photograph taken at a professional studio, many times located in the town where they resided.

117

Frank Merchant's Model T car is shown in this 1927 photograph with the new glass side window. The horse and carriage that had for many years been used for transportation began to be replaced by other means. (Courtesy of Don Lance.)

Ward W. Mount had photographs of the area, taken from the plane of Don Lance, reproduced into postcards to sell in his general merchandise store. Lance is in his plane hangar preparing for the flight to take Mount up for his picture-taking session. (Courtesy of Don Lance.)

Julia Cullen Chavoustie, wife of Earl Chavoustie, stands dressed for the light dusting of snow. Julia and her husband ran a farm in the Lyme area for 28 years. She worked for many years as head cook at the Chaumont High School and for Robert Purcell of Cape Vincent.

Jeannine Narrigan is shown as a child at the summer cottage on Main Street in Three Mile Bay. Narrigan is the daughter of Clarence and DeEtta Gordon. (Courtesy of Jeannine Narrigan.)

Perl Phelps (second from right) is shown with his family and children of his second wife, Edith Fredenburg Klock, from her marriage to Thomas Cady Klock. Her children were named Bessie, Blanche, Earl, George, Fred, Ned, Percy, Thomas Jr., and Viola.

Claude Rickett and daughter Marion sit on an old bench under a shade tree. Claude Rickett was a school bus driver for many years.

A group gathers on the Fourth of July holiday at the Rickett restaurant. Standing in the doorway from left to right are Toots Crouse, Bev Mason, Cathy Valin, and Bill Angel. Those in the front are not identified.

Eleanor Chavoustie, daughter of Earl and Julia Cullen Chavoustie, sits in a baby carriage of the 1920s. Eleanor's father was manager for the Richards Hotel in Three Mile Bay after he retired from farming.

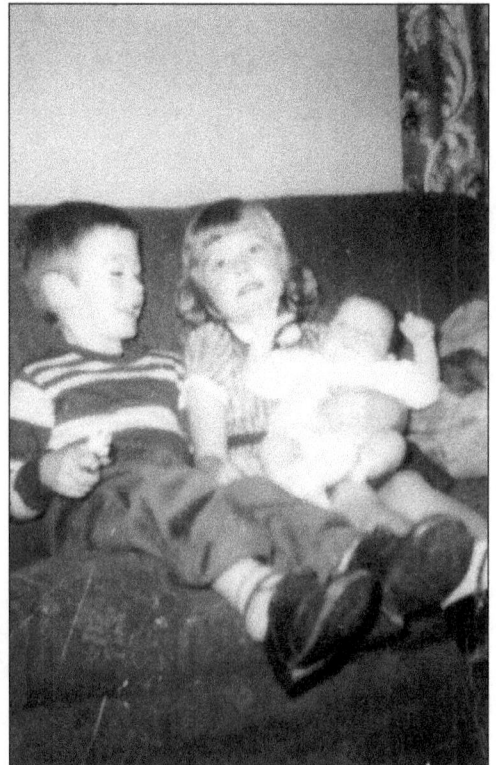

Bill (left), Alice, and Bruce Jackson, children of Anna and Earl Jackson, are shown at their home in the bay. Anna was the leader for the 4-H Club. Alice taught cooking lessons to some of the members for her mother. Their house was located on Main Street adjacent to the building that housed Earl's repair shop.

Diane and Terry Bourcy are the daughter and son of Marilyn and Paul Bourcy. The Bourcys ran a soda fountain across from Mount's general store in the Vincent building. Marilyn ran the business while her husband, Paul, was working at Fort Drum.

The members of the Klock and Northrop families are shown at a summer gathering. Included but not in order are some of the participants: Percy Klock, Earl Klock, Mary Klock, Ted Klock, Albert Klock, Blanche Klock, Pat Klock, Rosemary Klock, Joyce Klock, and in front, Ruth Klock.

Spencer Mount, son of Claude Mount, was employed at his father's general store before he purchased the business from his father. The post office, which originally had been located in the Barron Block, was relocated to the right section in the store building.

The building shown on the right was built by Earl Jackson after his discharge from World War II military service. He ran an automobile, marine, and general repair shop. He was the first Mercury dealer in Jefferson County. He closed his business and started work at Fort Drum. The school buses of Lyme Central School district were later housed in the building. Shown in the photograph are Francis Garrett, left, and David Wright.

Delos Flander operated a barbershop in his home at Three Mile Bay, bought hides for the Watertown Hide and Tallow Company, and worked as foreman on the town highway. Delos and his wife, Delia Rogers Flander, lived on the family homestead of Solon and Sarah Wood Rogers, parents of Delia. The homestead still stands.

Jeanne Hewitt Mitchell is shown in 1946 or 1947 while attending school at Plattsburg State Teacher's College. Mitchell moved with her family to Massachusetts. This is where she became a home economics teacher. Her final position before returning to the area was as a special education teacher in the Massachusetts area.

Friends gather at the local soda fountain; from left to right are unidentified, Paul Gosier, Pat VanNess, and Bev Wilkenson. Rickett's Restaurant, Bourcy's soda fountain, and the Town Tavern were frequented by many of the locals.

Children within many families often played together. Shown from left to right are Sandra Klock, daughter of Fred and Eleanor Chavoustie Klock, and cousins Sharon Chavoustie, Judy Chavoustie, and Robert Chavoustie, children of Francis and Rita Peters Chavoustie. (Courtesy of Judy Paro.)

Relaxing at a booth in the Rickett restaurant are Viola Klock (left) and sister Blanche Rickett, proprietor. Blanche worked as a Three Mile Bay rural mail carrier for 32 years. She did deliver the mail in rain and many times in raging snowstorms. When residents from the point needed supplies, Blanche would pack them into the car along with the mail for delivery.

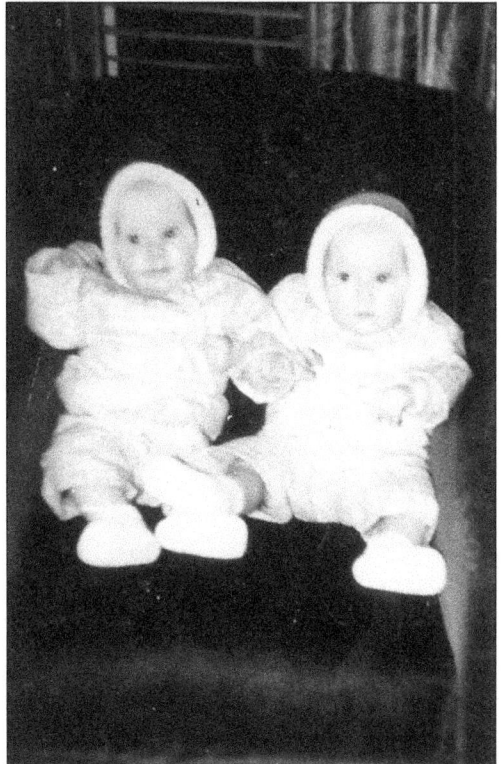

Twins Janet and Janice Chavoustie, children of Francis and Rita Peters Chavoustie, are shown at their home on the outskirts of Three Mile Bay. The Chavoustie family was large. Francis worked for many years at the Crescent Milling Company in Chaumont. (Courtesy of Judy Paro.)

Visit us at
arcadiapublishing.com

www.ingramcontent.com/pod-product-compliance
Lightning Source LLC
Chambersburg PA
CBHW080553110426
42813CB00006B/1294